T0132418

EVERYTHING WILL BE OKAY

A Compilation of Poems for Those Who Have Passed Away

Written and Illustrated by:

J.M.Gardner

Everything Will Be Okay
A Compilation of Poems for Those Who Have Passed Away

iUniverse books may be ordered through booksellers or by contacting:

iUniverse
1663 Liberty Drive
Bloomington, IN 47403
www.iuniverse.com
1-800-Authors (1-800-288-4677)

ISBN: 978-1-6632-0127-0 (sc)
ISBN: 978-1-6632-0128-7 (e)

Library of Congress Control Number: 2020909161

Print information available on the last page.

iUniverse rev. date: 05/20/2020

UNCONDITIONAL LOVE

This is for children of all ages, who need someone to hear.
It gives them understanding and takes away the fear.
We understand your pain; know how you feel is okay.
With every time that you wake, it'll be a better day.
There is a God in heaven, who won't give you more to bear.
Look to Him all the time; He'll show you that He cares.
He'll take you through your sadness and give you strength to grow.
He'll turn that pain and sadness to love that'll overflow.
The loved ones who have passed away will remain always in your heart.
They will always be in memories, and those memories will never part.

GOING UP TO HEAVEN

Going up to heaven is an honor for both big and small.
Everyone on this earth should know God loves us all.
When people die, they may be called up to meet Him.
All the angels will be at the gate to greet them.
Going up to heaven would be such a wonderful thing.
When you're there, there'll be no care.
Only joy it'll bring.

WHERE DID YOU GO?

I see your chair in your empty room.
Mom is sad, and Dad is filled with gloom.
No brother, no friend.
What have I done wrong?
Why do I have to grieve?
Dad said, "It's not your fault. He had to leave."
Just in your heart, you have to believe.
Even though you can't see him,
He'll always be there,
Especially in times of love,
Happiness, sadness, and despair.

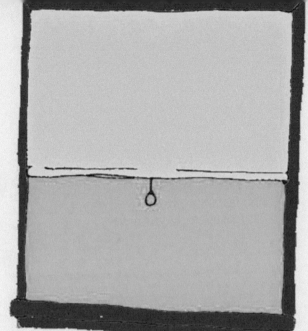
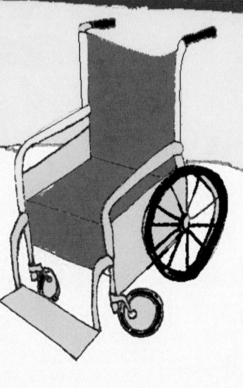
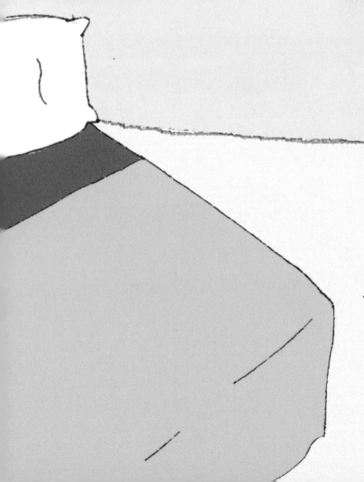

IN MEMORY OF GRANDMA

The scent of your perfume
Lingers in the air.
The warm smile you gave
Made us all feel so special and unique.
The strong words of wisdom from you
To the generations that later come,
The stride in your step,
Those times we cooked in the kitchen together,
Our most cherished encounters,
A glimpse of you in your Sunday best,
The unforgettable moments that I think of
As you transcend to a happier place.
I will always remember you, Grandma.

GRANDPA, GRANDPA

Grandpa, Grandpa,
Where did you go?
Will you come back?
I don't know.
Grandpa, Grandpa,
I miss you so much.
I miss your great strength
And your warm touch.
Grandpa, Grandpa,
You were the best.
Now as I see you,
We lay you down to rest.
Grandpa, Grandpa,
You were a good friend.
You will be missed
Until we meet again.

IT'S NOT YOUR FAULT

Mommy and Daddy know just how you feel.
We know, in time, your heart will heal.
Your loved one is gone, and it's not your fault.
Your whole world now comes to a halt.
Don't blame yourself—her time has just come.
Try not to remember the bad times
But remember the fun.
The sickness did come like a thief in the night.
But you must remember: she put up a good fight.

THE HEROIC SOLDIER, MY DAD

You were honored for your service.
It was so tried and true.
Never did we stop and think
That we would forever be missing you.
You risked your life to save so many,
Not knowing what would be.
I didn't really understand
That you weren't coming home to me.
I know you were a hero
And that you'll always be.
But in my heart, I'll see you as
The greatest dad to me.

A MOTHER'S LOVE

A mother's love is caring.
It's so warm and so unique.
It's like a long embracing,
Like a kiss on a baby's cheek.
It's so peaceful and serene,
As if in a warm cocoon.
Just knowing that her love is there
Can send you to the moon.
Some may ask this question:
Where is my mother's love?
Every time I look up to heaven,
Mine comes down from above.

IT'S OKAY TO CRY

When you're sad,
It's okay to cry.
It eases the pain to say goodbye.
You know the person is gone,
And it hurts so bad.
Once you cry,
You don't feel so sad.

REMEMBERING YOU

You meant so much to me.
You made me feel so good.
It was as if my world was taken
And no one understood.
I can't forget what happened.
And I will always know.
Everything we've been through

Will help me heal and grow.
I used to miss you dearly, but now I realize
That you are always with me
Even when I close my eyes.
I will never forget you.
You live here in my heart.
I remember when we were together,
Although now we're far apart.

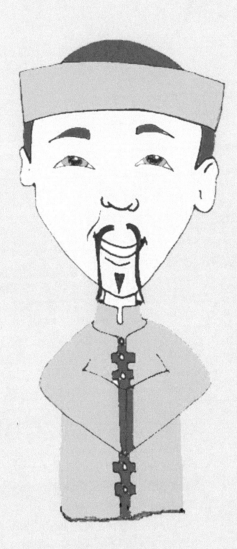

FOREVER LOVE

My uncle will be missed.
We were tight like glue.
He really loved his family,
But somehow we'll get through.
He always kept us smiling
And learning different things.
I'll remember all the lessons
And the joy he used to bring.
Now he's up in heaven,
Watching from the sky above.
One thing that I'll never forget
Is my uncle's love.

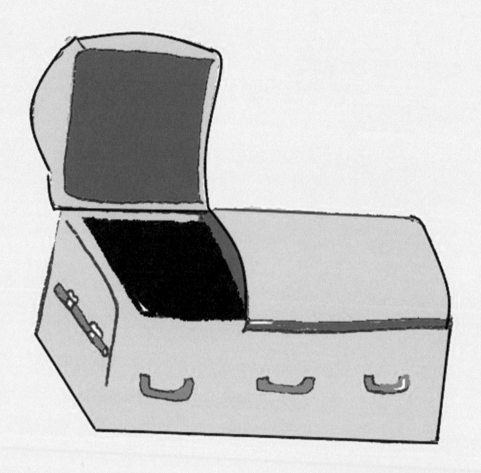

WHEN PEOPLE DIE

When people die, it's not so bad.
Sometimes it takes the pain they had.
When people die, where do they go?
Do they leave forever? I don't know.
When people die, does their love go away?
Or does it stay in your heart for a rainy day?
When people die, will we meet again?
We will meet in heaven in the end.

MY STAR IN THE SKY

My star in the sky shines bright for me.
My star in the sky makes me happy.
My star in the sky is filled with love.
My star in the sky is high above.
My star in the sky will always be there;
That's because my star in the sky is my father's care.

FOR MY SISTER

Those special times that we shared
Will be missed so very much.
Your sisterly advice that was given and your caring touch.
I think about you daily,
About what could've been.
I cry out for you all the time.
You were my best friend.
I carry you in my heart,
And everywhere I go,
I never want to forget
How much you loved me so.

IT'S OKAY TO BE AFRAID

It's okay to not know what's going to happen.
The end might not be so clear.
Your family is there to comfort you,
No matter how far or near.
In the end there might be sadness.
You might even be confused.
Now the overall outcome
Might give you the blues.
Be brave no matter what.
You must try to stay strong.
Keep your memories close to you
And know you can still go on.

MY AUNT'S DEPARTURE

It's so sad to see them crying.
We all miss her so.
My aunt, she died so suddenly;
We had no choice but to let her go.
I think about her often.
Sometimes I see her in my dreams,
Like an angel watching over me,
So peaceful and serene.
I know she's up in heaven,
Looking down from up above,
Giving her protection, her guidance, and her love.

THE SHOT

It came without a warning.
I was so very scared.
People started screaming, and no one was prepared.
Now there's one who's gone from that fateful day.
My cousin whom I dearly loved will never get to say,
"I love you" to his parents, because his life was lost.
All it took was that one shot, and now he's paid the cost.
He was just a baby riding on his bike.
Now one thing he'll never see is the rest of his life.
He'll never get to marry, have kids, or play with friends.
Because of that one bullet, his life came to an end.
The time we had was priceless, and memories will stay.
All I can do now is hope to see him again someday.

SAY A PRAYER

I will say a prayer for you
So you know that I love you.
I keep you in my heart
So you'll know my love is true.
I will say a prayer for you,
For you to keep me safe.
No matter where I go,
You will be in my special place.
So I say a prayer for you
To hold back all my tears.
That way you will be remembered
For many, many years.

SPIKE WENT AWAY

Spike was my dog and my very best friend.
He got sick, and we could never play again.
I miss him dearly, but I know that he's okay.
Because Spike was so old, he met his dying day.
Our memories will always be there.
Now I have a brand-new pet
To give my love and care.

TILLY THE CAT

Tilly the cat was my friend.
I loved her to the end.
Although she has passed,
Our love will last,
And, in time, my heart will mend.

DID YOU KNOW?

Did you know that he was sick?
Did you know I kind of knew?
Did you know it hurt for me to see
Him looking so sad and blue?
Did you ever try to tell me?
Or at least just fill me in?
Did you ever stop and realize

I was losing my best friend?
It would have made it easier
If I had known what was going on,
If you had told me what could happen
And that I should stay strong.
I would have felt much better
If you had filled me in.
I don't think I would've felt so sad
About losing a brother and a friend.

RIP

Does "rest in peace" mean forever
Or just until we meet again?
I know it can happen to anyone,
Like my family, a pet, or a friend.
I know it will be sad
To see loved ones leave,
Although sometimes it's for the best
And it's meant to be.
Especially if we don't get the chance
To even say goodbye.
I know they're in a better place,
And can now rest in peace.
Just knowing that makes me happy.
It puts my heart at ease.

Printed in the United States
By Bookmasters